My Report Card Tells On Me

by Teresa Short Mitchell
Illustrated by Sean Winburn

AuthorHouse™
1663 Liberty Drive
Bloomington, IN 47403
www.authorhouse.com
Phone: 1 (800) 839-8640

Published by AuthorHouse 08/30/2018

ISBN: 978-1-5462-5776-9 (sc)
ISBN: 978-1-5462-5775-2 (hc)
ISBN: 978-1-5462-5777-6 (e)

Library of Congress Control Number: 2018910297

Print information available on the last page.

This book is printed on acid-free paper.

authorHOUSE®

Key Vocabulary

enthusiasm	wondering	approaches	beaming
semester	progress	casually	extremely
interjects	consistently	sarcastically	reluctantly
dismissing	exchange	conference	interrupts

Curriculum Standards

For educational purposes, this book supports the following skills/ curriculum:

- ✔ Character feelings and emotions
- ✔ Compare and contrast
- ✔ Contractions
- ✔ Inflectional endings
- ✔ Parts of speech
- ✔ Problem-solving
- ✔ Quotations
- ✔ Settings
- ✔ Types of sentences
- ✔ Verb tenses

Jaida and Lissa are best friends. Jaida loves school and cannot wait to see her teacher, Mr. Johnson every day. Lissa hates school and cannot wait to go home every day. Like other mornings, Lissa and Jaida are sitting together on the school bus. Jaida excitedly says, "You know we get our report cards today!" Lissa asks, "Who cares?' 'Oh, I forgot… you!"

Jaida is in good spirits and does not let Lissa's attitude blur her enthusiasm for the day. She has worked hard this semester and cannot wait to get her report card. Her grandmother has promised her five dollars for every A and one dollar for every B.

Lissa is in a foul mood when they arrive at school. As they exit the bus, the counselor, Ms. Brown checks on Lissa as she does each morning to help her focus on learning. When Ms. Brown asks Lissa what is wrong, Jaida interjects and says, "Today is report card day and her report card is going to tell on her!" The counselor asks Lissa, "What is she talking about?" Lissa responds, "I hate school!"

Jaida in her upbeat mood says, "I love school. School is a wonderful place to be." Ms. Brown asks Jaida to share with Lissa why she thinks school is a wonderful place to be. Jaida begins sharing how she has a lot of friends at school. That she enjoys doing class work in groups and how she cannot wait to get home and tell her mother everything she has learned each day.

Ms. Brown reminds them that they can help each other. Lissa quickly shares that Jaida is a know-it-all. Ms. Brown responds, " No one knows-it-all because we all should be learning something new every day."

Jaida blurts out, "My teacher says I am smart, but I still have to work hard!" She looks at Lissa and says, "If I don't do my class work, my report card tells on me. If I don't do my homework, my report card tells on me." Lissa asks in a confused voice, "What does that mean?" Jaida says, "Well, if I do not do my class work or forget to turn it in, the teacher marks it down in her grade book." Lissa says, "So?" Jaida says, "So, she will tell my mom and there is no way I can get an A on my report card." Lissa says, "All you care about is getting A's." Jaida responds by saying, "My grandmother gives me a dollar for every B that I get too."

The counselor lets both of them know that she has heard enough standing in the hallway. This conversation needs to be held in private so she invites both of them to her office.

When they arrive and sit down, she asks Lissa if she completes and turns in her class and homework each day. Lissa responds by shaking her head side to side. Ms. Brown asks Lissa, "Do you think it is important for you to do class and homework?" Lissa shares, "My mind is on other things." The counselor informs Lissa that her parents go to work every day to provide clothing, shelter, and food for her. That is their job. Right now, going to school is her only job and she needs to do it well. She goes on to explain that her parents get a paycheck for doing a good job and she gets a report card that tells her parents whether she is working hard in school each day.

Jaida says, "My report card tells my mom and grandmother that I have been working hard." The counselor asks Lissa, "What do you think your report card is going to say about you?" Lissa softly whispers, "My report card is going to tell on me." Before dismissing them to class, the counselor tells them to come by her office before they go home so she can see their report cards.

All day long, Lissa is wondering what her report card will tell her parents. All day long, Jaida is asking the teacher, "When are you going to pass out report cards?"

After recess, Mr. Johnson begins calling each student to the kidney table to discuss their progress with their report cards. Jaida is third to meet with him. Mr. Johnson reminds Jaida of the goal she set for herself, "I want to make the Principal's List." He reviews Jaida's report card with her, asks and answers questions about her progress. Mr. Johnson tells Jaida that she should be proud of her report card because it says she consistently worked hard. He then congratulates her for making the Principal's List. Jaida is bubbling with pride as she and Mr. Johnson exchange a high five.

It is Lissa's turn to meet with Mr. Johnson. Mr. Johnson smiles at Lissa as she slowly approaches the table. Lissa casually sits down. Mr. Johnson asks Lissa to tell him how she thinks she did this grading period. Lissa says, "I don't know." Mr. Johnson tells her to think about it and asks her to share her goal. Lissa says sarcastically, "To be a better student." Mr. Johnson asks her to share the strategies they had discussed that would help her to become a better student. (Silence) Mr. Johnson asks Lissa if she believes that she has become a better student. There is more silence.

Mr. Johnson says, "Let's compare your grades for the first and second nine weeks." He shows Lissa her report card. "Can you show me any areas where you improved as a student?" Tears begin to well in Lissa's eyes and she exclaims, "You just don't like me!" Mr. Johnson says, "That is not true, Lissa. I care about you. I don't like that you do not want to do class work and refuse to return homework, but I like you as a person." Mr. Johnson places his hand on Lissa's shoulder and says, "I want you to do well, but you have to want to do well. You have to try. Unfortunately, your grades continue to drop and your report card tells your parents that you have not done any better since our conference."

Jaida blurts out, "Mr. Johnson, the counselor, Ms. Brown wants to see Jaida's and my report cards before we go home today!" "Yes, she told me, Jaida." Mr. Johnson allows them to get a counselor's pass and reminds them to come right back. Jaida is beaming and Lissa is feeling extremely low. While walking in the hall, Jaida says, "If you want to, we can study together." Lissa does not respond.

They arrive at the counselor's office, go in and have a seat. As Jaida shares her report card, the counselor smiles but does not comment. Then, Lissa reluctantly shares hers. The counselor asks Lissa if she had done her best. Lissa shakes her head from side to side. The counselor asks her if she believes the report card grades are accurate. She nods her head. The counselor tells her to use her words and reminds her that she is going to have to explain her grades to her parents.

Lissa says softly, "I could have done better. I could have tried harder." The counselor tells her that she is happy to know that she recognizes and can admit that. Jaida says excitedly, "I am going to get a whole lot of money today!" Lissa responds, "I want to be like Jaida." The counselor tells her that she doesn't need to be like Jaida or anyone else. She just needs to be the best Lissa that she can be.

"Well then,' Lissa says, 'next grading period, I am going to make Honor Roll because Jaida says we can study together." The counselor smiles and shares, "That is what friends do, they help each other." She adds, "This report card is not one to be proud of, but if you can verbally share with your parents how you plan to do better." Lissa interrupts. "I can see it now." "See what?" asks Jaida. "Next grading period, my report will tell some good things about me." "Mine too," says Jaida.

Printed in the United States
By Bookmasters